ISBN 978-0-365-06310-0
PIBN 11336553

For support please visit www.forgottenbooks.com

1 MONTH OF
FREE
READING

at

www.ForgottenBooks.com

By purchasing this book you are eligible for one month membership to ForgottenBooks.com, giving you unlimited access to our entire collection of over 1,000,000 titles via our web site and mobile apps.

To claim your free month visit:

www.forgottenbooks.com/free1336553

English
Français
Deutsche
Italiano
Español
Português

www.forgottenbooks.com

Mythology Photography **Fiction**
Fishing Christianity **Art** Cooking
Essays Buddhism Freemasonry
Medicine **Biology** Music **Ancient**
Egypt Evolution Carpentry Physics
Dance Geology **Mathematics** Fitness
Shakespeare **Folklore** Yoga Marketing
Confidence Immortality Biographies
Poetry **Psychology** Witchcraft
Electronics Chemistry History **Law**
Accounting **Philosophy** Anthropology
Alchemy Drama Quantum Mechanics
Atheism Sexual Health **Ancient History**
Entrepreneurship Languages Sport
Paleontology Needlework Islam
Metaphysics Investment Archaeology
Parenting Statistics Criminology
Motivational

BUREAU OF PLANT INDUSTRY
Horticulture

M. R. N.

VISITORS WELCOME

The Seven Acres are situated ten miles north of
Boston, on the White Mountain Road

TELEPHONE CONNECTION

L. N. DAVIS

Stoneham, Mass.

203 Main Street

1929 — GREETINGS — 1929

928 weather conditions were very unfavorable
rly part of the season for the flowers, the
w quite well and later we had some very
blooms. But as a whole it wasn't as good a
ear as could be; we trust that this year will
n make up for it.

nk the customers for their many letters telling
appreciation of the quality of our bulbs and
erful luck they had with them, many amateurs
first and second prizes, etc. We also wish to
escriptions of the flowers we use are largely
nators and trust they will be satisfactory.

ng you all for past patronage and trusting
s will continue to give you all great pleasure
ess.

With best wishes,
THE SEVEN ACRES.

INFORMATION

ifferent varieties of Dahlias we have abbrevi-
follows: Decorative, D.; Peony, P.; Cactus, C.;
Cactus, H. C.; Show, S.; Pom Pom, P. P.
he variety favors two different types, both are
ed.

arantee all bulbs and plants true to name and
e in good condition. If not satisfactory when
, notify us at once.

with order or in advance of shipment. **No
Orders.** Please state when you wish your order

ORDER EARLY

ese reduced prices some of the varieties will be
early; if no objection, we substitute something
or better at the same price.

G PLANTS ON THE NEWER VARIETIES AT ONE-HALF PRICE OF BULBS

NO PLANT LESS THAN $1.00

GROWING THE DAHLIA

ion: Open, sunny or partial shade. Cultivate
thoroughly. Plant from May 1st to June 20th.
ole one foot deep. Put in shovel of manure or
lant food. Cover with an inch of soil. If stake
e used, set in. Plant bulb four inches deep,
tally, and cover. Cultivate at least once a week.
water until the plants are well above the
When the buds appear water the plants thor-
once or twice a week. Apply any good fertil-
irring the soil lightly after. To obtain extra
owers, disbud freely, leaving only a few buds
inches on each plant.

plants should be planted TWICE AS DEEP
were grown in pots or 4 or 5 inches deep. They
be watered and shaded for a few days after
ɫ.

Bulb

e Whittier, H. C.—Large flower on good, strong stems, primrose yellow $2.5

alet, D.—A rich brown, producing many large flowers, very good habits 2.5

lon, D.—Here we have one of the very best new yellows, in shape, size, quality 7

State, D.—Very large cream yellow on long, strong stems, free bloomer and keeps its size until the end of season 1.0

Wilson, D.—Large orange red, tipped with gold, very showy 7

ck Jack, D.—Very large velvety maroon, with good stems 1.5

nie Brae, D.—Shaded blush pink, very large .3

no, D.—Large size flower on very strong stems, brown and copper color 4.0

r Claws, C—An immense American Cactus of ruby red 7

r of Lawrence, D.—Very large yellow 1.0

r of Peabody, H. C.—A very attractive flower of wine color with silver reverse 1.0

hing, D.—Scored 84 as an exhibition flower at American Dahlia Society Trial Garden. It is hard to describe this Dahlia, it is so different in color and formation from the average. The seven inch flower, on good stems, is a blending of cerise, old gold and yellow 1.0

orado, D.—A striking, large, gold Decorative, of the best habits 3.0

Granda, H. C.—An attractive flower of vivid orange 2.5

nor Vandeveer, D.—Beautiful rose pink on long, stiff stems, one of the best 7

tabeth White, D.—Rich combination of coral pink and salmon, amber glow at base of petals; prize winner 1.0

Cole, D.—Beautiful red and gold. Unusually large 2.0

. H. Carr, D.—Large, deep purple flowers eight inches. The best of its color 3

ry of New Haven, D.—Clear lavender pink, an exquisite shade. Very large flowers on strong stems 7

ridge, H. C.—Very good new white 1.5

den West, C.—Deep, rich yellow, heavily overlaid with orange. Good cut flower 5

ce Allen Fay, D.—Rosy crimson, darker in the center. Large well formed flowers on good stems 5

ry Sheldon, D.—Very large pink and white; great exhibition flower 1.0

en Hollis, S.—Deep scarlet; largest and best of its kind and color; good bloomer; very striking 5

ependence, D.—Large, well set up flower of mauve pink or lilac on strong stems 1.0

sey's Beacon, D.—Chinese scarlet, very large and attractive flowers on strong stems 1.0

Bulbs

Jersey's Mammoth, D.—Very large flower, golden mahogany 1.50

Jersey's Wonder, D.—Large orange yellow............ 3.00

Jim George, D.—A most beautiful garnet velvet, large and good habits 1.00

Judge Langford, D.—Large, rich pansy purple, of good habits .... .75

Lady Alla, P.—Bright scarlet, long strong stems. Fragrant. Very attractive .... .35

Le Grand Manitou, D.—Royal purple splashed white, sometimes clear purple .... .35

Mahogany, C.—Good size flower on good stem, dark velvet red 1.00

Maid Marian, H. C.—Something different in formation, large, rose pink with curled and twisted petals 2.50

Marmion, D.—A monster in every way, size, habits, stem and quality, golden yellow with bronze suffusion, none better 3.50

Massachusetts, D.—Awarded Certificate of Merit by American Dahlia Society and Dahlia Society of California. Winner of many first prizes. The color is a gorgeous shade of amaranth purple, the tight center petals pansy purple, outer petals shading Syrian rose. Immense flowers on good stems, splendid for exhibition 1.50

Miss California, D.—Beautiful new color, Oriental fuchsia, good stem, style and size 2.00

Mrs. Eleanor Martin, D.—Beautiful mulberry, giant flower, good for exhibition 1.00

Mrs. Frank Dunbar, D.—This beautiful new Dahlia is a most charming shade of clear lavender. The formation is perfect. The stems are long, strong and straight, holding the flower well above the foliage 1.00

Mrs. Geo. W. Jenkins, D.—Certificate of Merit. Flower is very large, bright, rich scarlet, the foliage exceptionally good. Always attracts attention 1.00

Mrs. I. DeVer Warner, D.—An immense flower of exquisite mauve pink, on long, strong stems .... .35

Mrs. H. D. Young, D.—Pure old gold flowers on long, strong stems, very free bloomer 1.00

Mrs. J. K. Allen, D.—A very attractive flower, color is red at base of petals with buff to the tips 1.00

Nancy Davis—A new formation for the Decorative Dahlia, having a very high or thick appearance caused by the large number of petals growing so close to each other. The color is a gold, shaded darker at the tips which come out to a point, making it seem like a Hybrid, which always comes double to the end of the season 2.00

Bulbs

Nature's Masterpiece, D.—A new Oregon Dahlia of special merit, color combination of old rose, cinnamon and metalic bronze with violet reflex on reverse of petals; extra long strong stems which hold the large blooms above the foliage 3.50

Our Country, D.—Wonderful large flower of deep purple, always tipped white. Most unusual and attractive .... .75

Pacific Sunset, P.—Large, salmon buff, on strong stems 1.00

Perella, D.—A good size flower on good stems, pink 3.00

Polar Snow, D.—Beautiful white decorative, full flower ....:......... .35

Pop Stewart, D.—Large pure lilac-pink flowers on strong stems 1.50

Pride of California, D.—Large red decorative that cannot be beaten .... .35

Primula Rex, D.—Very large, well formed flower, cream color 3.50

Queen of the Garden Beautiful, D.—One of the largest of all, primrose yellow on strong stems 3.00

Radio, D.—Very large, blood red, edged and tipped yellow. Good for exhibition 1.00

Regina Coeli, D.—Was awarded a Certificate of Merit. A beautiful white Dahlia; formation of the flower puts it in a class by itself. We have received enthusiastic letters from customers stating it to be all that we claimed it to be 1.00

Robert Treat, D.—American Beauty shade. The flower is of perfect formation with long, strong stem .... .75

Rodman Wanamaker, D., P.—Golden bronze and salmon pink. This is one of the largest and most beautiful Dahlias on the market; grand for exhibition or garden purposes 1.00

Rolo Boy, H. C.—Very large amber on strong stems 1.00

Roman Eagle, D.—Large exhibition flower of brilliant copper, nice formation 1.00

Rookwood, D.—Pure bright cerise rose, immense flower, splendid straight stems, free bloomer 1.00

Sagamore, D.—This is good for exhibition or cut flowers; golden yellow, good size 1.25

Senorita, D.—Rich velvety crimson, blooms held erect on strong stems, measures 9 to 10 inches across. A prize winner .... .75

Seven Acres No. 6, P.—Beautiful flower on the popular autumn shade of amber and gold. The flower is very heavy for a peony, the tall plants are covered with blooms on long, strong stems, which hold the flowers erect. It is exceptionally good as a garden variety 1.00

Bulbs

Seven Acres No. 37, D.—The vivid orange red seems a magnet to focus the eye and closer inspection brings forth exclamations of delight. The reverse of the orange red petal is gold, the whole flower being brilliant and colorful. A large, heavy flower, with great depth, bound to win popularity 1.00

Seven Acres No. 44, H. C.—Certificate of Merit at the American Dahlia Society Trial Garden. The flower is of unusual formation, with long and twisted petals. The color is a shade deeper than Jack Rose. The plants are covered with blossoms on long, strong stems all the season. It is a good Dahlia for massing in the garden and for a cut flower 1.00

Sorris Souvenir, H. C.—Large, clear yellow 1.00

Shirley Brown, H. C.—Large apricot and gold, long stems .... .75

Sanhican Gem, D.—Old rose 1.00

Shudow's Lavender, D.—Silvery lavender, slightly shaded white. Large flower, long stiff stems, free bloomer 1.50

Snowdrift, D.—Giant, pure white, best for garden .35

St. Bernard, D.—Soft, creamy white, suffused clear pink. Good stiff stem. Beautiful exhibition variety .... .75

Susan G. Tevis, D.—Deep shade of lilac, bluish sheen. Very unusual and striking flower .... .75

The Bashful Giant, D.—Apricot shading gold. Mammoth flower, good for garden and exhibition .... .35

The Bandit, H. C.—Large flower on very strong stems, of very unusual coloring, being made up of three colors, spectrum red, reverse, buff, yellow, with twisted petals 2.00

The Crysler, D.—A beautiful new pink which blooms on top of the stem. Large flowers on strong stems, free bloomer 3.00

The Eagle, H. C.—Sulpher yellow, large flowers, good keeper. Long, stiff stems, very prolific .35

The Emperor, D.—Very large maroon colored flowers on strong stems .... .75

The Surprise, D.—This is one of the best of the new ones. Very large, deep and good stems; mulberry or rose wine color 1.50

The Telegram, D.—A very large golden yellow, heavily tipped white, on long, strong stems 1.50

Trentonian, D.—Very large, finely formed flower of coppery bronze or Indian red 1.00

Uncle Tom, D.—Very dark velvet of good size and shape 2.00

Violetter, H. C.—Very unusual colored flower, good habits 1.00

White Court, H. C.—A large white, loose petals of very attractive formation 1.00

Washington City, D.—White flower and good habits .... .35

Winter Time, C.—A very good white (C.) of good habits 1.00

Bulbs

Wonderland, D.—Large chocolate maroon with silver reverse 2.50

World's Best White, D.—Large white on strong stems 1.00

POM POMS EACH 25 CENTS

Alwine—White tipped lavender

Ariel—Orange buff, beautiful cut flower, good bloomer

Belle of Springfield—Brick red

Bobby—Plum color, another favorite

Catherine—Beautiful yellow, free bloomer

Frau Emie Heneck—Pink, good free bloomer

Gretchen Heine—Blush white, rose tips

Highland Mary—Wine, white shadings, long stems, best cut flower

Snow Clad—Pure white, very good

Joe Felet—White

The following varieties are only in moderate supply. Will quote prices if interested.

Nancy Sue Lang, H. D.—Immense flower, red, tipped gold, very attractive

Shirley E. Shattuck, D.—Large, attractive lavender on strong stems

Gracias, D.—Large flower of yellow, heavily overlaid with red

Eagle Rock Jewel, H. C.—Cream, overlaid cameo pink, large flower on strong stems

Eagle Rock Beauty, H. D.—Large, refined flower, pink and cream color, good stems

Harry Mayer, D.—Very large lilac purple on long, strong stems

The Boy Scout, H. D.—Very large flesh pink, lighter at center, very classy flower

Silverado, H. C.—Long, white petals, shaded lavender, covered with silver sheen

Walheim Sunshine, D.—Very large golden yellow of good habits

Jersey's Gleam, D.—Very free blooming Dahlia, medium size, coral pink, very good habits for garden varieties

My Maryland, H. C.—Very stylish flower on good stems, pink lavender

Regal, D.—A very prolific, large, beautiful colored, bloom of autumn, bronze and old rose colors

Starlight, H. D.—Very large, pure gold on strong stems; new, will be one of the best for a long time

Alexander Pope, H. P.—Large shaggy red

Barber Redfern, D.—Large flower on strong stems, old rose and gold

Berengaria, H. D.—Many large flowers of orange and gold color

Elsie Daniels, D.—Large pale violet orchid on good stems

Zeus, H. C.—Large flower, glowing red tipped gold

W. J. Irwin, D.—Very large lavender purple, strong stems

Selbach's White, D.—Very prolific, white, fine for cut flowers

Paul Revere, D.—Very large velvet red

Grace Burnett, H. C.—Dark velvet red on strong stems

Fort Monmouth, H. C.—A giant flower of very good habits, brilliant crimson maroon, very good

Santa Anna, D.—Salmon rose and gold, large, classy flower, good stems

THESE POPULAR VARIETIES
50c each; $5.00 per dozen

Acquitana, H. C.—Salmon pink
Arbonita, D.—Lavender pink
Ambassador, C.—Yellow buff
Amun-Ra, D.—Copper orange
Azalea, D.—Cream yellow
Ballet Girl, C.—White-orange
Bridal Veil, C.—White
Cardinel Mercier, P.—Blush pink
Charm, D.—Burnt amber
Chester Gordon, P.—White
Cigarette, C.—White and orange
Della V. Potter, D.—Large lavender
Elizabeth Slocomb, D.—Garnet
Elsie Oliver, H. C.—Creamy pink
Georgeous, P.—Yellow and scarlet
Geo. Walters, H. C.—Salmon pink
H. A. Hyde, D.—Cerise and white
Jane Selby, D.—Mauve pink
Jersey's Beauty, D.—Beautiful pink
Judge Parker, D.—Golden buff
Judge Marean, D.—Salmon, orange and red
Junior, D.—Large lavender
Kalif, H. C.—Large red
Kitty Dunlap, D.—Carmine rose
Lake Erie, D.—Large lavender
F. W. Fellows, C.—Orange and scarlet
MacGregor, H. C.—Spectrum red, good
Marina Graves, D. P.—Brilliant yellow
Marion Weller, D.—Beautiful pink, good
Mariposia, H. C.—Pink and violet, good
Mephistopheles, H. D.—Vivid scarlet
Millionaire, D.—Large lavender
Minamoto, H. C.—Velvet scarlet
Moll Pitcher, D.—Crimson and white
Mr. Crowley, D.—Glowing salmon
Mrs. E. L. Lindsey, D.—Gold and scarlet
Mrs. Ethel Smith, H. C.—Large, creamy white
N. C. 4, D.—Scarlet and cream
Paul Michael, D.—Orange and buff, good
Rosa Nell, D.—Bright rose
Sequoia Gigantea, D.—Yellow
St. Francis, D.—Cream
Sampson, D.—Combination of gold and red
The Giantess, D.—Immense, amber, good
William Slocomb, D.—Large, canary yellow
Winfield Slocomb, D.—Orange, good

25c each; $2.50 per dozen

Acquisition, S.—Rich lilac
D. N. Moore, D.—Velvet maroon

Duzon, D.—Brick red
Jack Rose, D. S.—American beauty
J. M. Goodrich—Salmon, tipped go
Maud Adams, S.—White, tinted pinl
Mrs. C. Turner, H. C.—Yellow

POM POMS ....each 2

GLADIOLI

Albania—Very large, pure white .
Alice Tiplady—(Prim) orange ....
Crimson Glow—Deep crimson ....
Delphi—New shade of pink ....
Diana—Bright red ....
Evelyn Kirtland—Beautiful pink .
Europa—Large, pure white ....
Gold—Golden yellow ....
Gretchen Zang—Soft pink ....
Halley—Salmon pink ....
Herada—Pure mauve ....
Mrs. Frank Pendleton—Light pink
    blotch in throat ....
Mrs. Francis King—Light scarlet .
Mrs. F. C. Peters ....
Mrs. Watt—American beauty shade
Mary Pickford—Creamy white .....
Peace—Large white, lilac throat .
Pearl—Pink, creamy throat ....
Prince of Wales—Early blooming
Purity—White ....
Purple Glory—Deep velvet maroon
Scarsdale—Lavender ....
Schwaben—Yellow, very large ....
Scribe—Tinted white, streaked cri
Willibrink—Flesh pink ....
Yellow Hammer—Pure yellow ....
Giant Nymph—Large, light pink .
Jewel—Pink, yellow throat ....
Nora—Light violet lavender ....
Rose Ash—Ashes of roses ....
1910 Rose—Rich rose, white lines

MIXED GLADIO

$3.00, $4.00, $5.00 per l
Special Collection, 25 f
35c, 50c, 75c, $1.00 pei

SPECIAL COLLECT

Described Elsewh

Special Collection (No.

Bashful Giant	Lady A
Maud Adams	Pride o
J. M. Goodrich	Augustı
Mrs. Charles Turner	Mr. H.
D. N. Moore	Snowdr
Bonnie Brae	Judge I

Special Collection (No. 2) $3.50

Geo. Walters	Sequoia Gigantea
Bashful Giant	Geo. H. Carr
Bonnie Brae	Mr. H. A. Hyde
Snowdrift	Mrs. I. De Ver Warner
Judge Parker	William Slocomb
Pride of California	Lady Alla

Special Collection (No. 3) $4.00

Our Country	Della V. Potter
Jersey's Beauty	Rosa Nell
Amun Ra	Elsie Oliver
Judge Parker	MacGregor
Winfield Slocomb	Lake Erie
William Slocomb	Kitty Dunlap

Special Collection (No. 4) $4.50

Mariposa	Ambassador
Junior	Ballet Girl
Judge Marean	Cigarette
Eagle	Paul Michael
N. C. 4	Mrs. Lindsay
Mr. Crowley	Gorgeous

Special Collection (No. 5) $5.00

Robert Treat	Cushing
The Giantess	Mrs. J. K. Allen
Our Country	Mrs. H. D. Young
Avalon	Elizabeth White
Marion Weller	Senorita
Ellinor Vandeveer	Harry Sheldon

Special Collection (No. 6) $7.50

Rodman Wanamaker	City of Lawrence
Jim George	Our Country
Ellinor Vandeveer	Bay State
Elizabeth White	Robert Treat
Massachusetts	St. Bernard
Harry Sheldon	Mrs. Frank Dunbar

Special Collection (No. 7) $10.00

Trentonian	Jim George
The Telegram	Elizabeth White
The Surprise	Jersey's Beacon
Roman Eagle	City of Lawrence
Jersey's Mammoth	Independence
Massachusetts	White Court

Special Collection (No. 8) $15.00

The Bandit	Maid Marian
Eva Cole	Amulet
Uncle Tom	Pop Stewart
Nature's Masterpiece	Selbach's White
Jersey's Wonder	Alexander Pope
Elkridge	Independence

Special Collection (No. 9) $25.00

Bueno	The Bandit
The Crysler	Eva Cole
Harry Mayer	Maid Marian
Jersey's Gleam	Selbach's White
Jersey's Wonder	Grace Burnett
Nature's Masterpiece	Perella

DAHLIA BULBS

We offer our surplus bulbs from $1.00 to $25.00 per dozen, OUR SELECTION. These values are unsurpassed, as they comprise a surplus of most varieties in the catalog, and any of the collections are worth twice as much as you pay. We tag all bulbs, except the $1.00 and $2.00 collection. We guarantee satisfaction, and will endeavor to give as wide an assortment of colors and types as possible.

DAHLIA LABELS. PAINTED COPPER WIRE

40c per 100; $1.75 per 500; $2.50 per 1,000, net

SEPARATING THE CLUMP

Cut stock close to bulbs, turn clump upside down and put strong knife or hatchet in the center, pound it until you make two halves. Avoid breaking neck of bulb. Then take hock or straight knife and cut off bulbs, being sure they have an eye, leaving on as much crown as possible.

A pair of canvas gloves with the right thumb heavily taped will be a help.

KEEPING THE BULBS

By L. N. Davis

There are almost as many opinions as there are growers on keeping the tubers over the winter. This is perfectly right, as every cellar is different, and this means a decidedly different method for storing and preserving one's bulbs.

First of all, I would suggest that everyone keep a thermometer in the cellar, for only in this way can you tell how hot or cold it is.

Now the bulb itself must be taken into consideration. Is it large or small? Has it a tendency to decay easily, or maybe to dry or shrivel up to almost nothing? This is the time when the evil of overfeeding for large flowers in the summer becomes apparent. If you take several clumps of good bulbs, all the same kind, put them in storage in the same box, in a short time, the clump that has been forced or fed heavily will begin to decay, or, if small sized, will dry up, while those grown without any food will be found O. K.

Next to be considered is the cellar where the bulbs are stored. Generally the old fashioned, dirt bottom cellar, without heat of any kind, is almost perfect. About the only care for these bulbs is to pile on the floor and cover with burlap bags if they show any signs of wrinkling or drying up.

In a cellar with a small amount of heat, pack the bulbs in boxes or barrels, lined with newspaper and cover top with more paper. Watch for a few weeks after packing, and if they start to mildew near crown, take off top paper and give the moisture, which is always coming out of the clumps, a chance to escape.

In a cellar of 45 degrees or 50 degrees, or warmer, with cement bottom and heater, the bulbs will need more protection from the hot, dry air. Pack in shallow boxes, about 8 inches high (vegetable bushel boxes

perfect) and cover with shavings or sawdust. Look
the bulbs four times during the storage period,
vember 30, January 1, February 22, and April 1. If
y are in good condition, they can be packed away
in, but if they have started to decay, cut off all the
ayed parts and apply powdered sulphur or air slack-
lime to the parts that have been cut.

n a very warm, dry cellar with cement floor, where
temperature goes from 45 to 65 and even in the
d storage closets of such cellars where more or less
t will get in, the following treatment has proved
cessful. The bulbs when dug should be placed at
e in shallow boxes (if the earth isn't too wet or
gy.) Do not shake the dirt from the clump and,
er placing in the box, fill in with more loam, not
deep, about 6 inches. Set boxes on or near the
r. If lack of space compels you to place boxes on
of each other, be sure to put wooden braces be-
en the boxes, to prevent resting tightly on top.
culation of air is necessary to keep the moisture es-
ing from the tubers.

ou can see that the keeping of bulbs rests wholly
h the individual and his cellar conditions. The
iosphere in every cellar is different, even with the
ne heat. If you have had success your way in
ring, my advice is don't change. But if you haven't
i good luck keeping bulbs, try one of the other ways.
lbs can be successfully wintered if you find out
ir cellar conditions, then treat them by the methods
gested. Remember, if one man can keep them over
winter, you, too, should be able to do the same.
ours for better luck in storing.

Member of
American Dahlia Society
New England Dahlia Society
Dahlia Society of California
Massachusetts Horticultural Society

Lightning Source UK Ltd.
Milton Keynes UK
UKHW020757270219
338009UK00008B/1768/P